MACMILLAN
MUSIC and YOU

Barbara Staton, Senior Author
Merrill Staton, Senior Author
Marilyn Davidson
Susan Snyder

Macmillan Publishing Company
New York

Collier Macmillan Publishers
London

AUTHORS

Barbara Staton has taught music at all levels, kindergarten through college, and for eight years was music television teacher for the State of Georgia. She is author of a four-volume series of books and records designed to teach music concepts through movement. She holds a B.S. degree in Music Education and an M.A. in Dance and Related Arts. Mrs. Staton has written numerous songs for television and recordings and is a composer member of ASCAP.

Dr. Merrill Staton earned his M.A. and Ed.D. degrees from Teachers College, Columbia University, and is nationally known as a music educator, choral conductor, singer, ASCAP composer, and record producer. He has been music director of and has conducted the Merrill Staton Voices on many network TV series and recordings. Dr. Staton has been a leader in the field of music education for over thirty years, and pioneered the use of children's voices on recordings for education.

Marilyn Copeland Davidson has taught music for over thirty years at all levels and is presently teaching elementary general music in Pequannock, New Jersey. She also teaches graduate music education courses. She holds a B.S. degree from Ball State University in Muncie, Indiana, a diploma from the Juilliard School of Music, and has completed the Master Class level of Orff-Schulwerk. She has served as national vice-president and president of the American Orff-Schulwerk Association.

Dr. Susan Snyder has taught general music for over twenty years. She holds a Ph.D. in Curriculum and Instruction and an Orff Master Teacher's Certificate. She has worked with preschool and handicapped children and has done extensive study in aesthetics, early childhood, and the Kodály approach. Currently, Dr. Snyder is teaching in the Greenwich, Connecticut, public schools. She is an adjunct faculty member of Teachers College, Columbia University, and Director of the Ridgewood Summer Courses, Ridgewood, New Jersey.

Cover Design and Illustration: Heather Cooper
Text Illustration: Randy Chewing, Len Ebert, Hima Pamoedjo, Jan Pyk, Lane Yerkes.
Photo Credits: CLARA AICH: 10B, 11TL, TR, 16, 17, 51. ART RESOURCE, NY: Scala, 42. THE BETTMANN ARCHIVE, INC.: 35. THE IMAGE BANK: © Robert Phillips, 10T. PHOTO RESEARCHERS, INC.: © Porterfield-Chickering, 45. © Ulrick Welsch, vii. THE PHOTO SOURCE: 20. PHOTOTAKE: © Yoav, 10C. VICTORIA BELLER SMITH: 4, 5, 23, 26B, 27T, 30, 36, 37, 39. MARTHA SWOPE PHOTOGRAPHY, INC.: 30B, 50. SUZANNE SZASZ: iv, 1, 26T, 27B.

Macmillan Publishing Company
866 Third Avenue
New York, N.Y. 10022
Collier Macmillan Canada, Inc.

Printed in the United States of America

ISBN: 0-02-295000-1   9 8 7 6 5 4 3 2

contents

UNIT 1
We Make Music iv
Who Laughs the Loudest? 2
Listen 3
High and Low 4
Steady Beat 5
Music Helps to Tell a Story 6

UNIT 2
Listening for Loud and Soft 8
Long and Short 10
Playing High and Low 12
What Sound Does Each Make? 16
Walking Home 18

UNIT 3
Look, Hear, and Move 20
Point the Beat 21
Play the Beat 23
Say It Fast and Slow 24
One Sound on Each Beat 26

UNIT 4
Same and Different 28
Sound and No Sound 32
Long and Short Sounds 33
Picturing Sounds 34

UNIT 5
The Strong Beat 36
Pitches 38
Peter and the Wolf 40
Two Sounds in a Beat 42
Reading Rhythms 43

UNIT 6
A New Friend 44
More Rhythms to Read 47
Beats in a Phrase 49

UNIT 7
What Do You Hear? 50
The Brass Family 51
Placing Pitches 52
Rain Sounds 54

UNIT 8
Sets of Beats 56
Form 57
Old and New Friends 58
Practice Rhythms 60

We Make Music

You can use your voice four ways.

This is my **talking** voice.

This is my **whispering** voice.

Who laughs the loudest?

2

Listen

loud

soft

High and Low

HIGH

LOW

Steady Beat

Music Helps to Tell a Story

high

middle

Listening for Loud and Soft

bow wow

meow

quack quack

Long and Short

Playing High and Low

High

Low

13

Town Ball

What Sound Does Each Make?

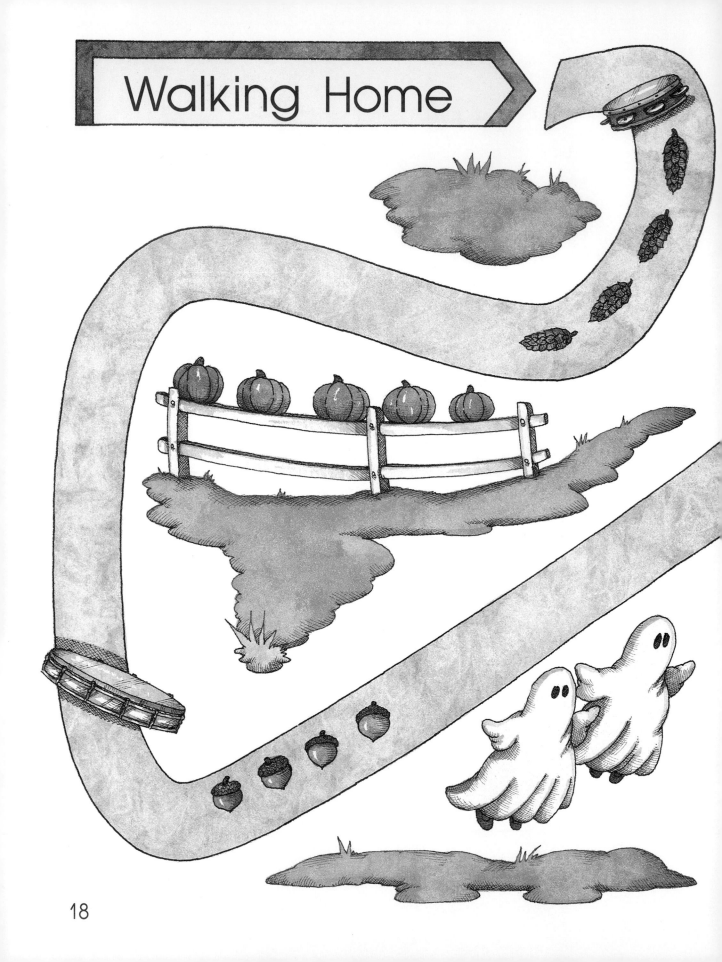

Walking Home

Look, Hear, and Move

Point the Beat

● Point to the dog on each beat.

● Point to a bird on each beat.

Play the Beat

● Play the beat.

Say It Fast and Slow

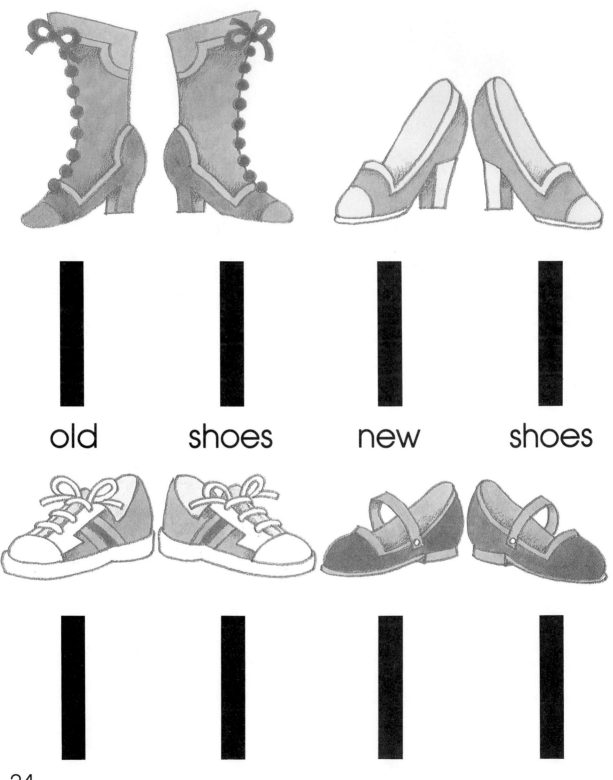

old   shoes   new   shoes

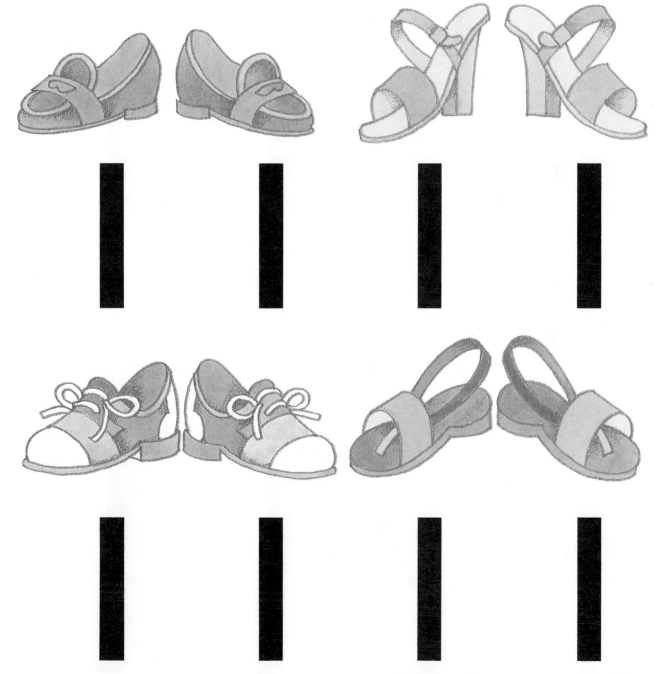

One Sound on Each Beat

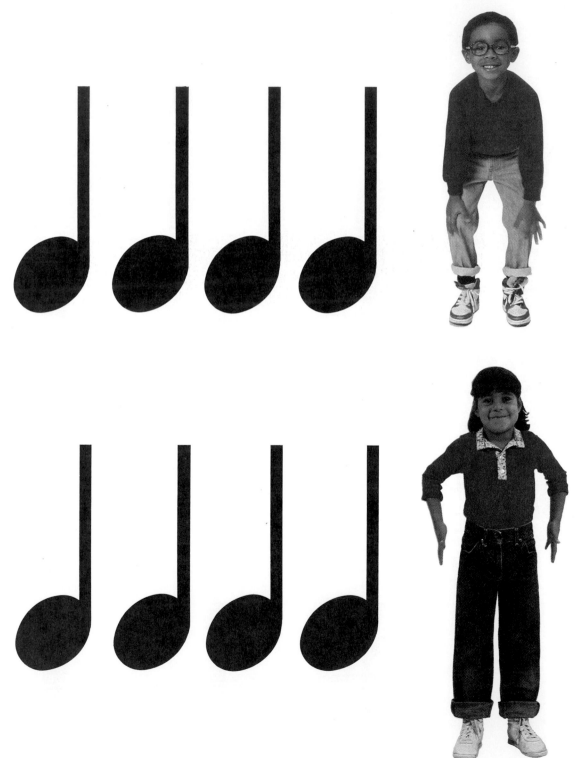

Same and Different

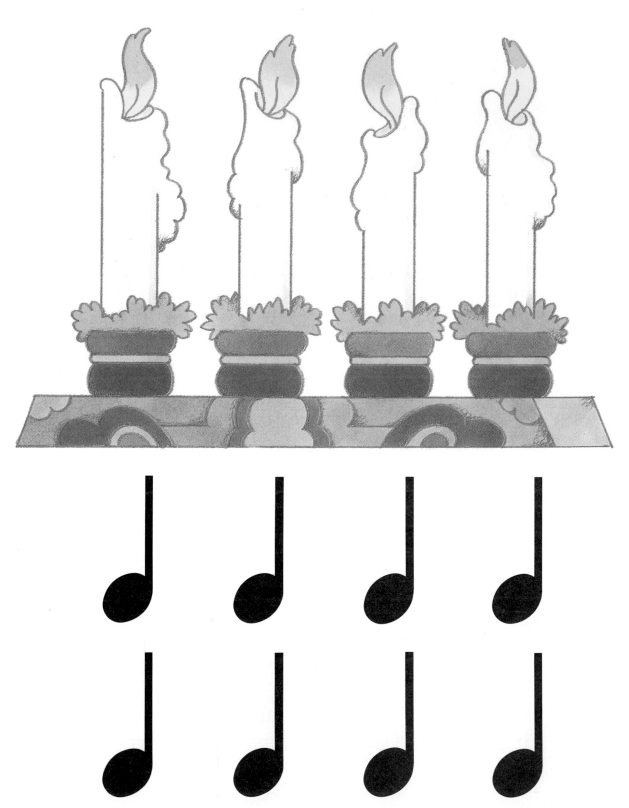

See what you hear.

piccolo   flute   cello   violin

Chinese Dance

Sound and
No Sound

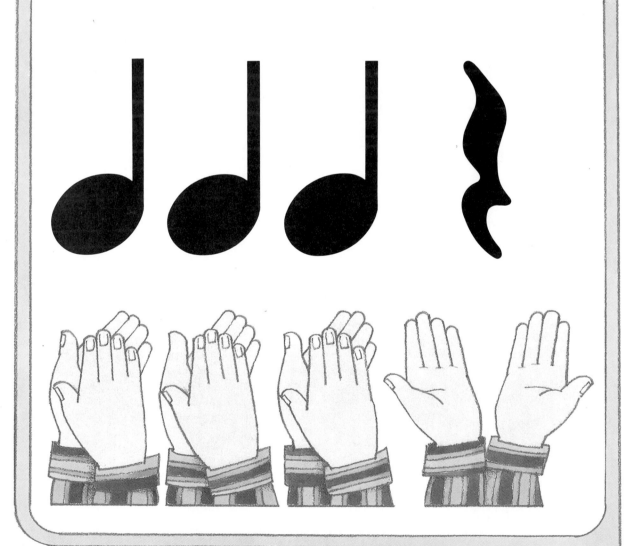

Long and Short Sounds

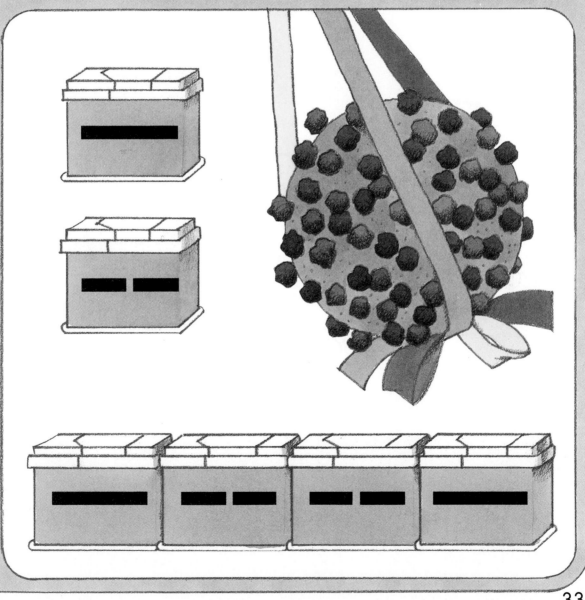

Picturing Sounds

so   mi   so   mi

Up on the Housetop

"Merry Christmas to All and to All a Goodnight," illustration to Clement Moore's
'Twas the Night Before Christmas, THE BETTMANN ARCHIVE, INC.

The Strong Beat

Pitches

The pitches stay the same.

Wake   me

F

The pitches go down.

Gold - en Gate

Peter and the Wolf

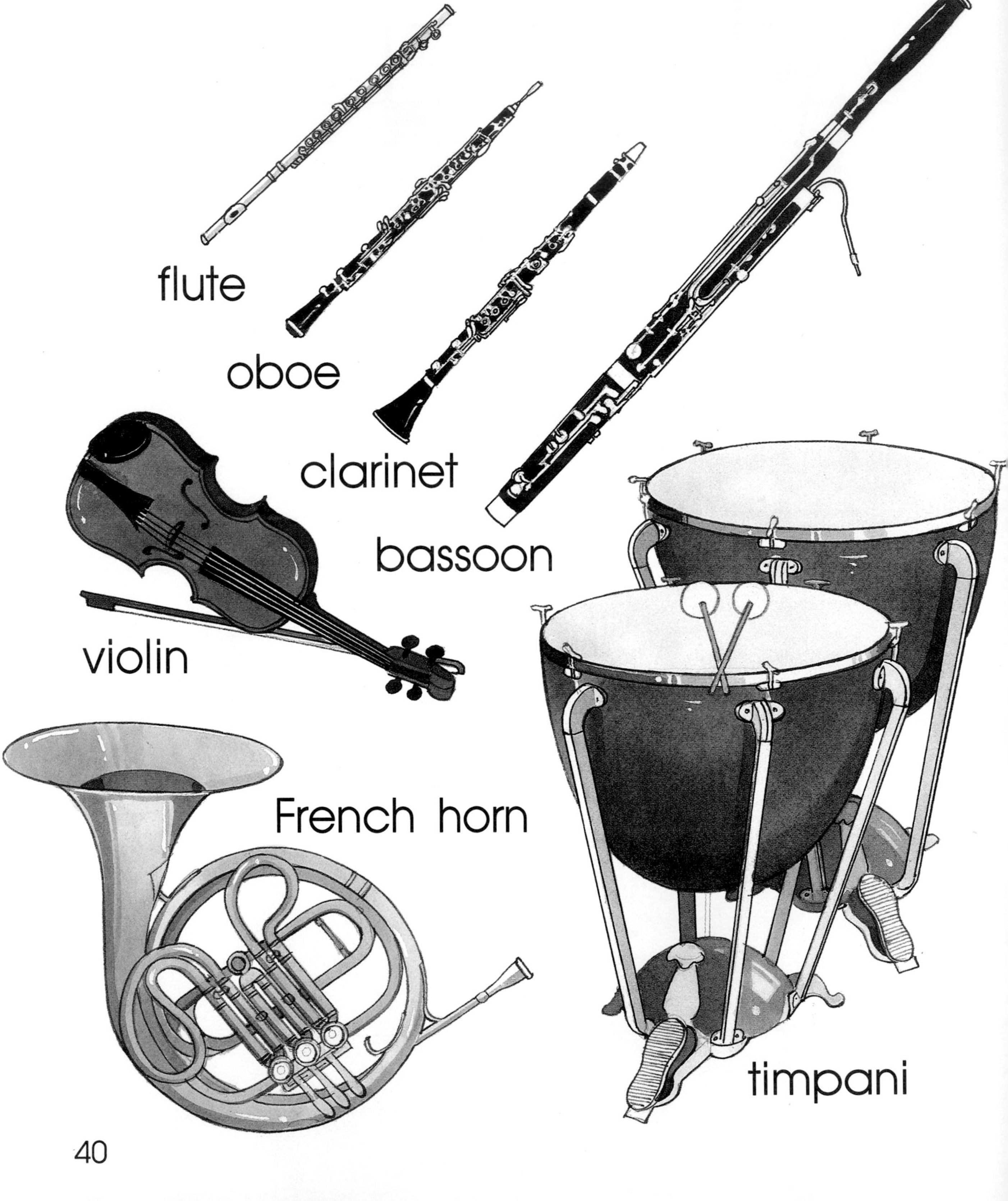

flute

oboe

clarinet

bassoon

violin

French horn

timpani

Two Sounds in a Beat

● Tap the rhythm.

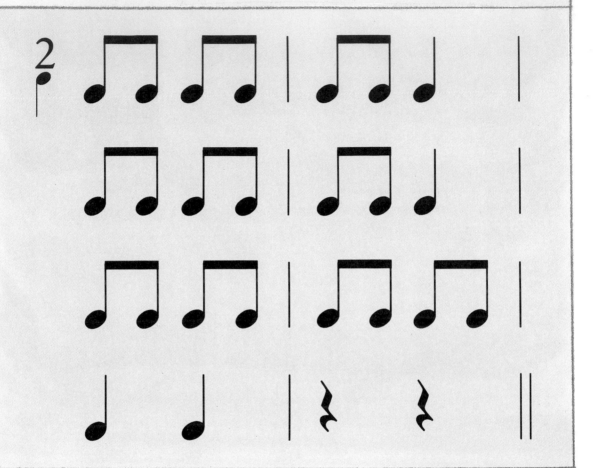

Reading Rhythms

● Tap another rhythm.

hot   cold   old

43

45

You can place notes.

around a line

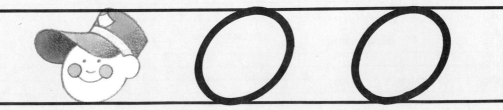

in a space

More Rhythms to Read

- Say these rhythms.

- Say *friend* for ♩

- Say *happy* for ♫

- Say *bell* for ♩
- Say *horses* for ♫

Bell Horses

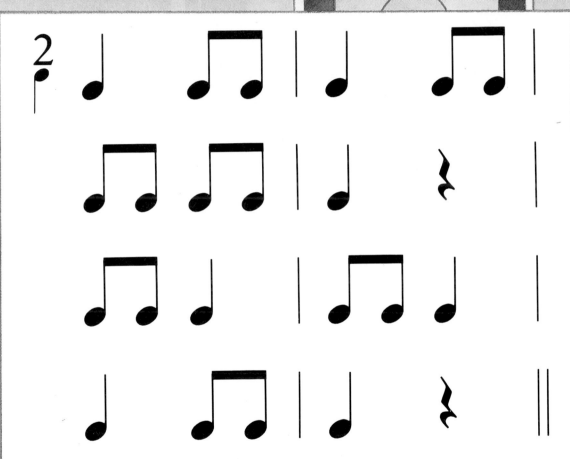

- Find *so.*
- Find *la.*

Beats in a Phrase

How many beats are in each **phrase**?

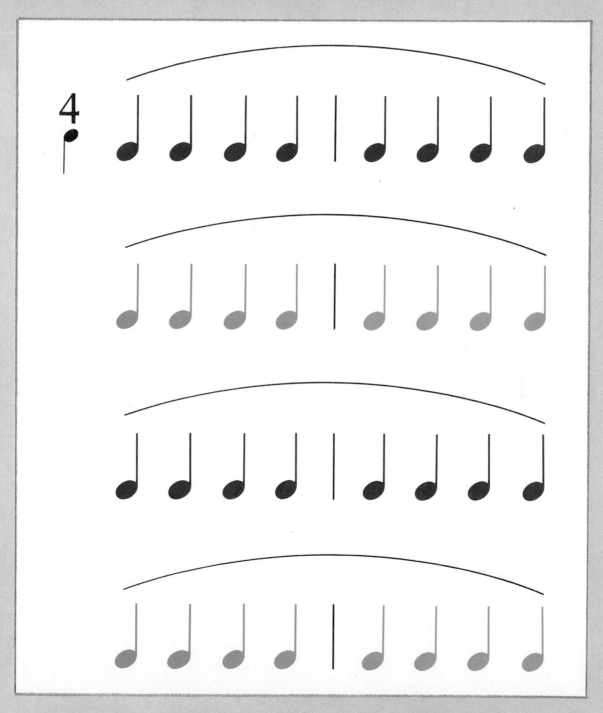

What Do You Hear?

Who will buy a broom here? Buy my brooms.

Which do you hear?

The Brass Family

- How are these the same?
- How are these different?

trumpet

trombone

tuba

French horn

Placing Pitches

When

so is in a space

mi is always in the space below *so*

and

la is always around the line above *so.*

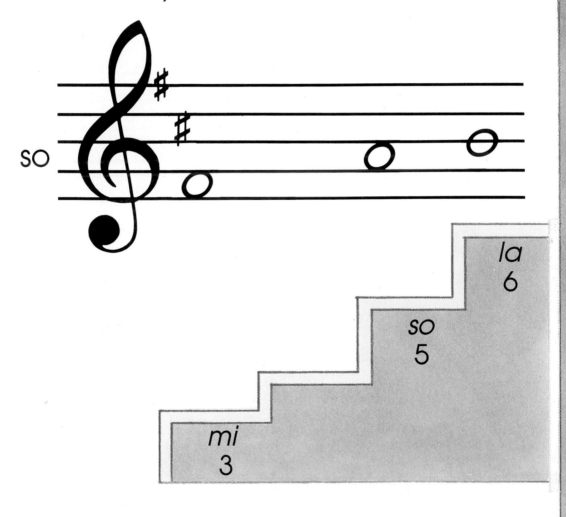

When

so is around a line

mi is always around the line below *so*

and

la is always in the space above *so.*

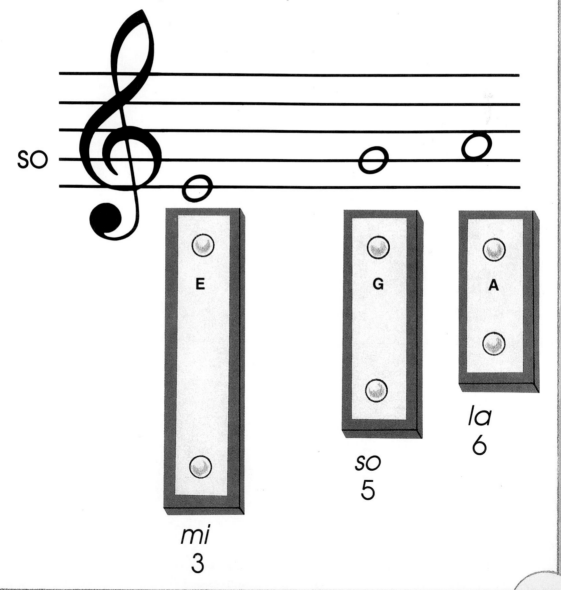

SO

E

mi
3

G

so
5

A

la
6

Rain Sounds

- Say *rain* for ♩
- Say *falling* for ♫

Rain, Rain Go Away

so

Rain, rain, go a - way,

Come a - gain an - oth - er day.

Rain, rain, go a - way.

All the chil - dren want to play.

Sets of Beats

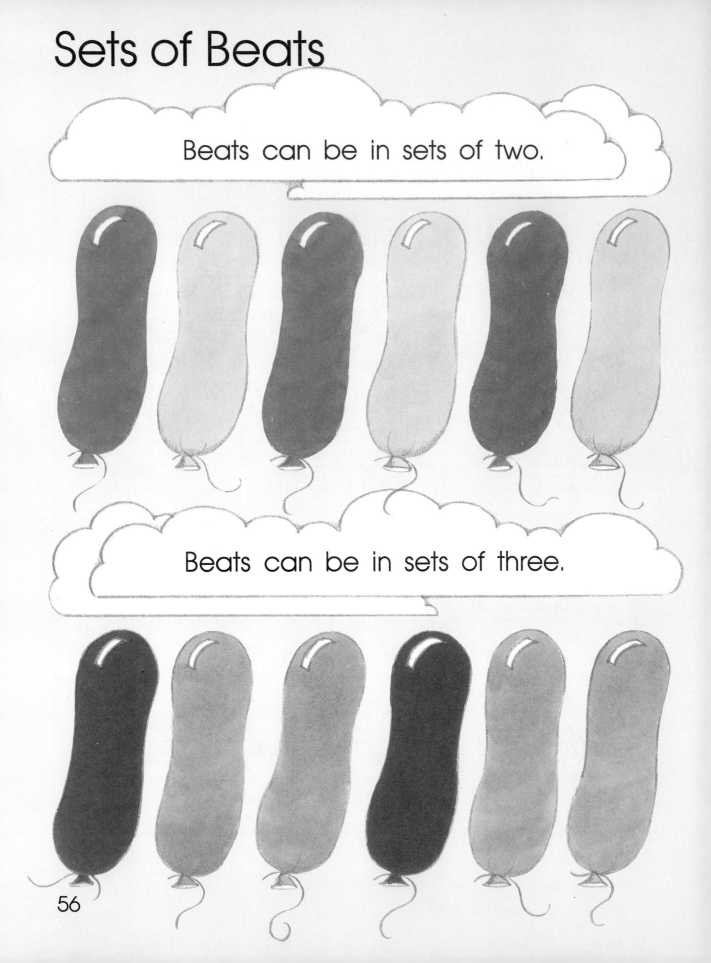

Beats can be in sets of two.

Beats can be in sets of three.

Form

Some music has two parts.

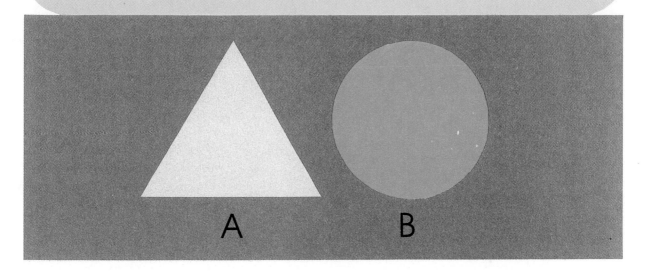

A   B

Some music has three parts.

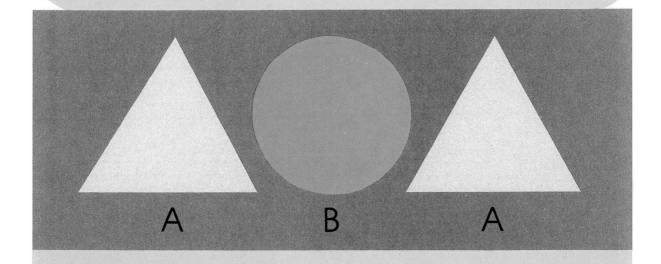

A   B   A

The order of the parts is called **form**.

Old and New Friends

- Read this song.

- Say *nine* for ♩

- Say *number* for ♫

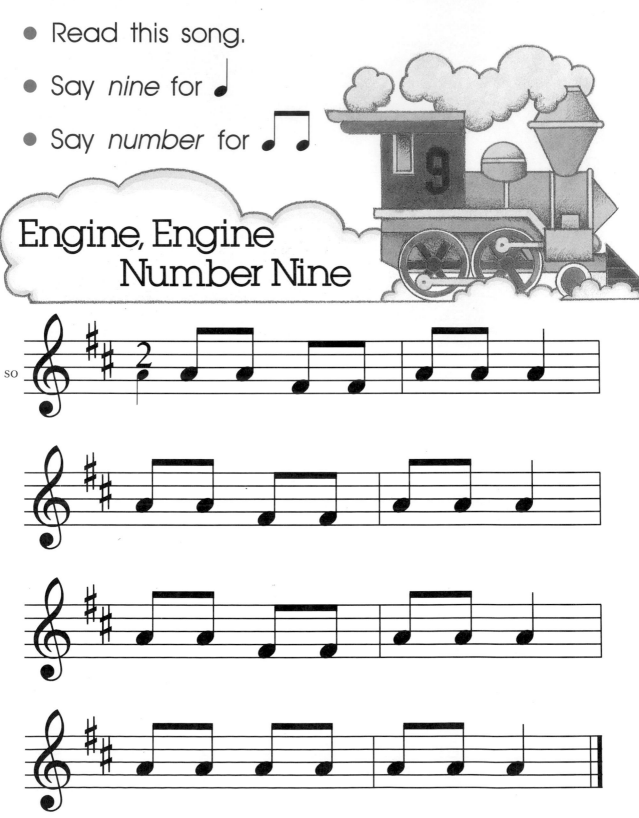

**Engine, Engine
Number Nine**

- Count each *do* in this song.

  How many can you find?

do	mi	so	la
1	3	5	6

Mouse Mousie

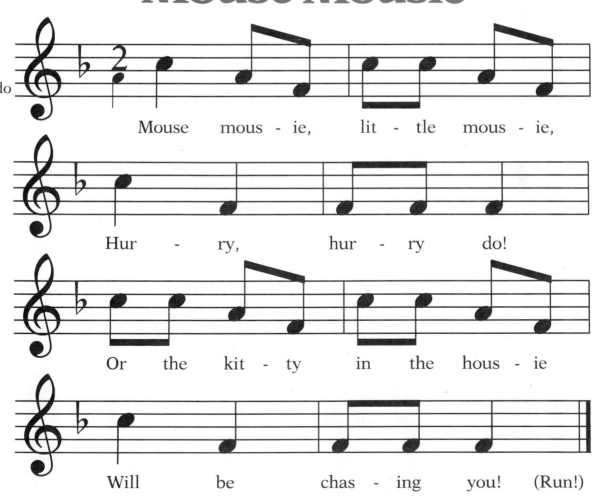

Mouse mous - ie, lit - tle mous - ie,

Hur - ry, hur - ry do!

Or the kit - ty in the hous - ie

Will be chas - ing you! (Run!)

59

Practice Rhythms
LOOSE TOOTH

I had a loose tooth, a wig-gly, jig-gly loose tooth,

I had a loose tooth, hang-ing by a thread.

So I pulled my loose tooth, this wig-gly, jig-gly loose tooth, And

put it 'neath my pil-low and then I went to bed. The

fair-ies took my loose tooth, my wig-gly, jig-gly loose tooth, So

now I have a quar-ter and a hole in my head.

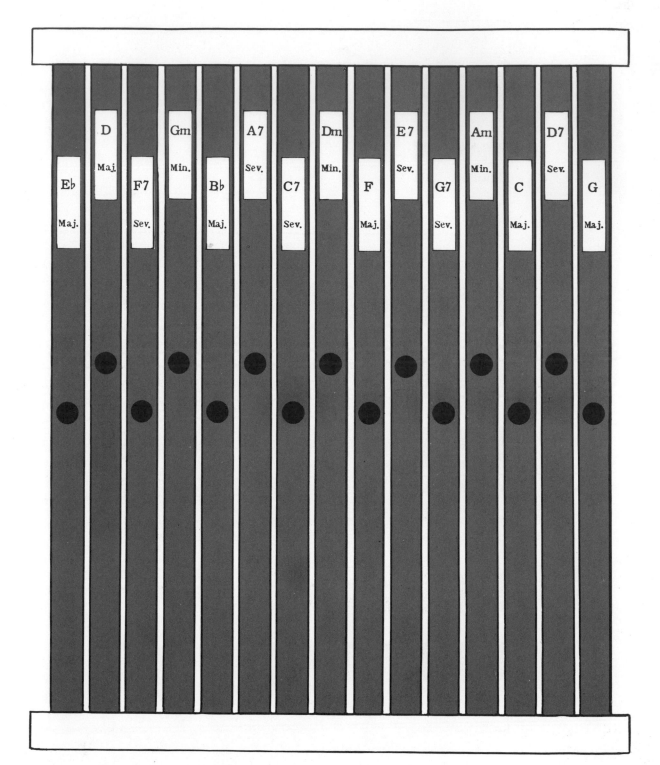